presents

THE CHOCOLATE EGG WILLOW

written and illustrated by

cathy gagliardi

Carnelian Moon Publishing Inc.

Ontario, Canada

carnelianmoonpublishing.com

Copyright 2020 by Cathy Gagliardi, Twinkling Lynx, twinklinglynx.com.

All rights reserved. This book or any portion thereof may not be reproduced or used in any manner whatsoever without the express written permission of the author except for the use of brief quotation in a book review.

Printed in the United States of America

ISBN: 978-1-989707-19-7

eBook ISBN: 978-1-989707-20-3

To All The Magical Children Who Make The World Shine!

"Hello friends, my name is Yumyum.

Would you like me to tell you a story?"

The Grand Old Bunny

thought it would be funny

to
wake up
at dawn,

and hide eggs on the lawn,

but with the sun so high,

they started to fry.

"What a mess!" he sighed.

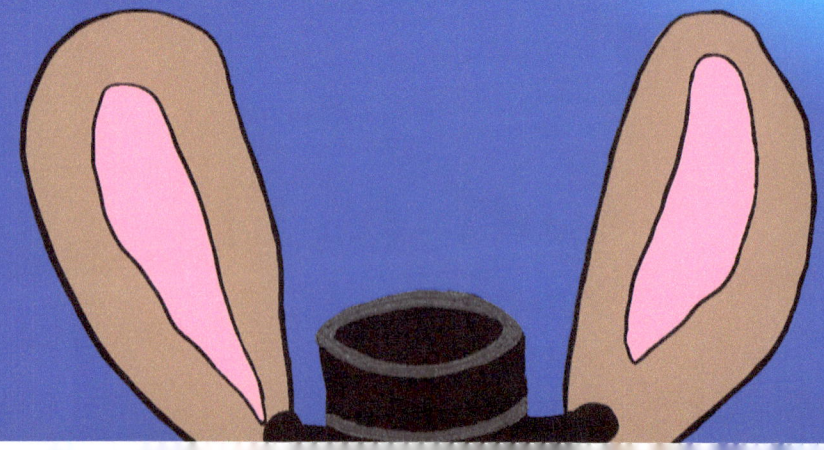

As folks came around,

trees started to grow.

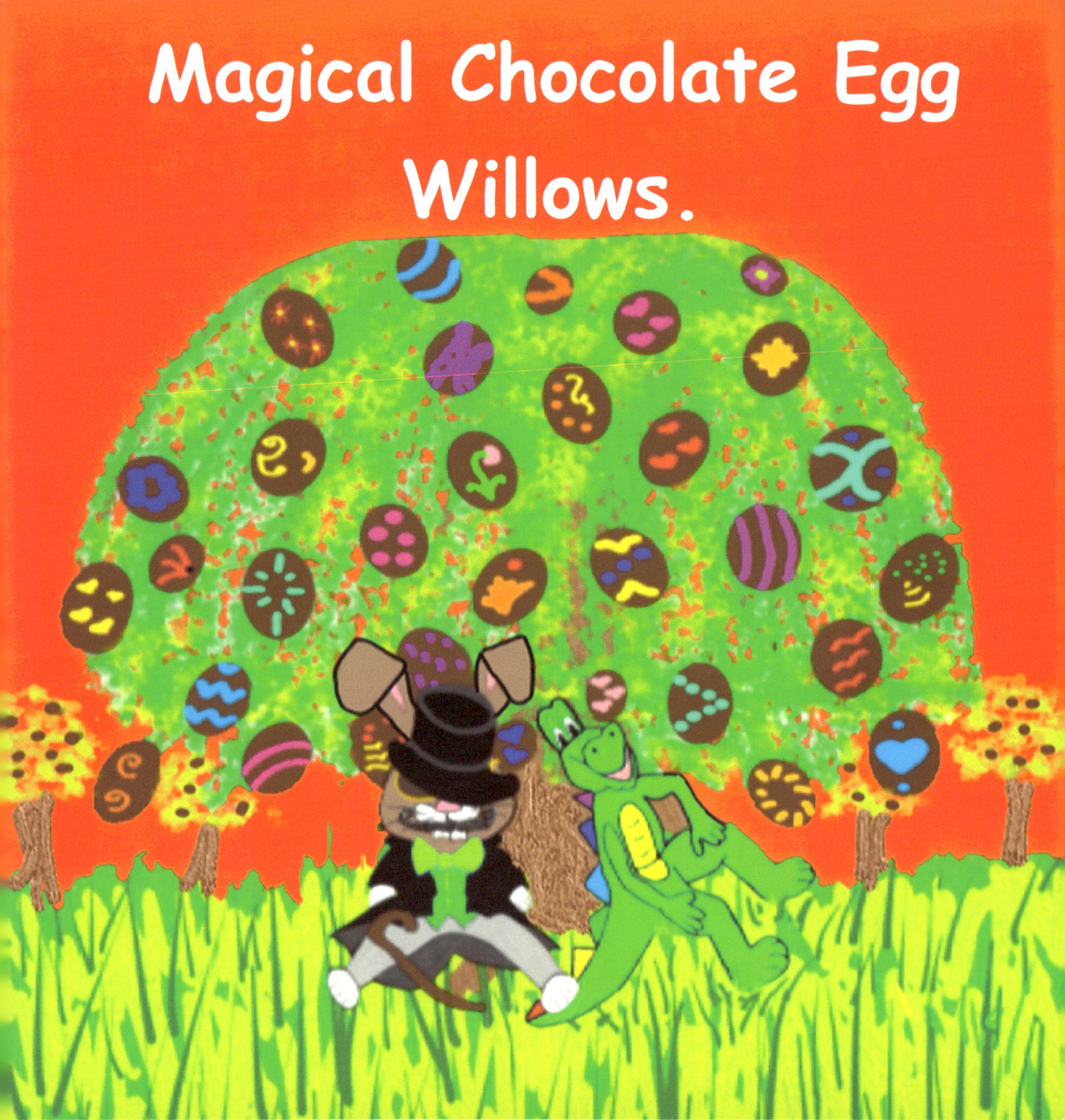

Magical Chocolate Egg Willows.

About the Author

Cathy Gagliardi of Twinkling Lynx is passionate about writing stories for children. She loves to visit schools and organizations around the world, including hospitals that work with children and has great joy in reading her stories.

She loves speaking with children and helping them to express their feelings of anxiousness, nervousness, being scared, or sad more easily. This is exactly what the Yumyum books have been created to do and she is so happy when someone buys one of her books for their children, or grandchildren.

Cathy believes that if young children learn these tools so well that as they grow, it becomes a natural response to anxiety or any feelings that they struggle with.

Cathy's vision is to have her books in the hands and homes of children and schools around the world! She invites you to join her by supporting her Go Fund Me Initiative at **twinklinglynx.com#GoFundMe** and support children around the world in receiving Cathy's books.

Other Books by Twinkling Lynx

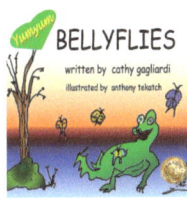
BELLYFLIES
Young Billy learns ways of tackling his anxious feelings with the help of his friend Yumyum the alligator.
Spanish version also available.
0-4yrs

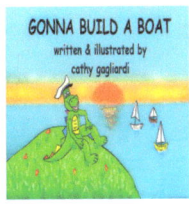
GONNA BUILD A BOAT
Yumyum the alligator and his friend Billy go on an adventure including friends along the way. Sharing a feeling of compassion, pride, conquering boundaries, contributing together to build a boat.
Spanish version also available.
0-6 years

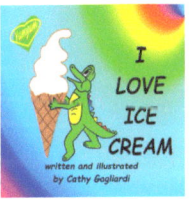
I LOVE ICE CREAM
Yumyum the alligator is excited to show an intrigued little girl how loving ice cream is the same as loving all people, all animals, and our amazing world.
0-4 yrs

MOTHER LOVE
Discover with Yumyum the alligator how big Mother Love is and how we are all a part of everything as you do the actions and have some fun.
0-4 yrs

Watch out for more Yumyum adventures to come. Check out TwinklingLynx.com and READ ALONG on the TwinklingLynx YouTube channel.

www.ingramcontent.com/pod-product-compliance
Lightning Source LLC
Chambersburg PA
CBHW041100070526
44579CB00002B/24